T0082316

LEVEL **3** READER

EVERYTHING AWESOME" ABOUT DANGEROUS DINOSAURS

WRITTEN AND ILLUSTRATED BY

MIKE LOWERY

Scholastic Inc.

To William and the Hauns
—M.L.

All rights reserved. Published by Scholastic Inc., *Publishers since 1920.* SCHOLASTIC and associated logos are trademarks and/or registered trademarks of Scholastic Inc.

Special thanks to Dr. Diego Pol, paleontologist, for his guidance and expert verification of the information included in this book.

Photos ©: cover, 1 left: propstore.com/Shutterstock; cover, 1 right: Goran Bogicevic/Alamy Stock Photo; back cover: Francois Gohier/Science Source; 4: Francois Gohier/ardea.com/www.agefotostock.com; 5: Puwadol Jaturawutthichai/Alamy Stock Photo; 7: Leonello Calvetti/Science Photo Library/Getty Images; 9: Francois Gohier/ardea.com/www.agefotostock.com; 11 top: Bernard Weil/Toronto Star via Getty Images; 11 bottom: Goran Bogicevic/Alamy Stock Photo; 12 left: E.R. Degginger/Alamy Stock Photo; 12 center: Holger Hollemann/picture-alliance/dpa/AP Images; 12 right: Francois Gohier/ardea.com/www.agefotostock.com; 17: AP Photo/Mary Altaffer; 18 top: LittleLazyLass/Wikimedia; 18 bottom: propstore.com/Shutterstock; 19: Kevin Schafer/The Image Bank/Getty Images; 21: Kabacchi/Flickr; 23: Lanzellotto Antonello/AGF/www.agefotostock.com; 25: Carl Court/Getty Images; 27: Andrew Rubtsov/Alamy Stock Photo; 31 top left: Rafael Trafaniuc/Shutterstock; 31 top right: Xavier ROSSI/Gamma-Rapho via Getty Images; 31 bottom: Richard Greiner/EyeEm/Getty Images; 32: Francois Gohier/Science Source.

ISBN 978-1-339-00031-2

10 9 8 7 6 5 4 3 2 1   23 24 25 26 27

Printed in the U.S.A. 40
This edition first printing, 2023
Book design by Doan Buu

TABLE of CONTENTS

What Is a Dinosaur?   4

How to Tell If It's a Dinosaur   6

What's for Dinner?   8

Dinosaur Traits   10

Giant Dinos!   14

Horned Dinosaurs   18

Armored Dinosaurs!   20

Tyrannosaurus Rex!   22

Dinosaur Brains   24

Even More Dinosaurs!   26

Extinction: What Happened?   28

Digging for Bones   31

WHAT IS A DINOSAUR?

THAT'S EASY! THEY'R UM...

A BIG... LIZARD THING?

DINOSAURS

WERE A GROUP OF PREHISTORIC, WARM-BLOODED REPTILES THAT RULED EARTH FOR MILLIONS OF YEARS.

Triceratops
(try-SERR-ah-tops)

SOME ATE MEAT.

SOME WERE SMALLER THAN CHICKENS.

SOME HAD HORNS!

SOME WERE AS BIG AS AIRPLANES.

Yummy!

SOME ATE VEGGIES.

SOME HAD LONG NECKS.

AND THEY WERE ALL AWESOME!

Tyrannosaurus
(tie-RAN-oh-SORE-us)

WHAT DOES "PREHISTORIC" MEAN?

GOOD QUESTION.

PREHISTORIC means anything that happened or existed in the time before we started keeping written records.

HOW TO TELL IF IT'S A DINOSAUR.

USE THIS HANDY CHECKLIST!

☑ 1. DINOSAURS LIVED DURING THE MESOZOIC ERA.

THE MESOZOIC ERA LASTED FOR ABOUT 180 MILLION YEARS. THE PLANET WAS MUCH WARMER THEN.

WHEN WILL AIR-CONDITIONING BE INVENTED?!

HE'S JUST KIDDING.

The Mesozoic era started roughly 251 million years ago. Dinosaurs ruled for a lot of that period, but they definitely weren't the only animals around.

☑ 2. DINOSAURS ONLY LIVED ON LAND.

THIS WASN'T A DINOSAUR!

NOT DINO

THEN... WHAT AM I?

AND WHAT ABOUT THOSE AWESOME SWIMMING MONSTER THINGS?!

Pterodactyl
(terr-oh-DACK-til)

Plesiosaurus
(PLEE-see-uh-SORE-us)

✗ NOT A DINO

☑ 3. DINOSAURS HAD BACKBONES.

Dinosaurs had spines! There's even a dinosaur named Spinosaurus, which means "spine lizard." The Spinosaurus had long spines on its back. These spines were called a "sail."

☑ 4. DINOSAURS WALKED WITH THEIR LEGS UNDER THEIR BODIES LIKE BIRDS.

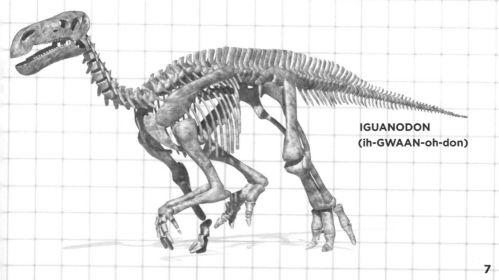

IGUANODON
(ih-GWAAN-oh-don)

WHAT'S FOR DINNER?

DINO DINNER

WHAT DID THE DINOSAURS EAT?

MENU
1 MEAT
2 VEGGIES

SOME DINOS ATE MEAT (CARNIVORES), AND SOME DIDN'T EAT MEAT (HERBIVORES).

SOME ATE BOTH. → OMNIVORES

MOST DINOSAURS WERE HERBIVORES.

They would eat leaves, small sticks, and seeds. An herbivore dinosaur's teeth weren't very sharp, and they were usually straight and close together, like a cow's teeth. Herbivores used their teeth to rake leaves and bark into their mouths.

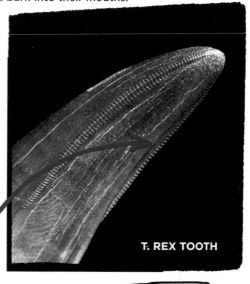

T. REX TOOTH

CARNIVORES

Dinosaurs that ate meat had long and sharp teeth that were serrated (which means they had edges like this). The serrated teeth helped them cut through the thick skin of their prey, including lizards, insects, mammals, and other dinosaurs.

AWESOME FACT!

Some dinosaurs would eat rocks that would end up in their gizzards. These rocks would help break down some of the stuff they ate to make it easier to digest.

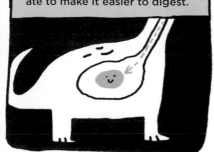

JOKE ALERT!

WHY DID THE HERBIVORE CHEW UP THE FACTORY?

BECAUSE IT WAS A PLANT EATER.

DID DINOSAURS

You might not like the answer to this one. We love to imagine a mighty T. rex standing over the top of a recent kill, making a loud roar to let everyone know how awesome it is. Well, scientists believe that the fearsome T. rex was actually a scavenger and would eat animals it would find that were already dead. And to take T. rex down yet another step, there's a chance...that it

DID DINOSAURS HAVE FEATHERS?

YES! WE KNOW AT LEAST SOME DINOSAURS HAD THEM!

Even if they had feathers, *most* dinosaurs probably couldn't fly. Maybe some could fly a little, but nothing compared to today's birds. The feathers were probably used for insulation or attracting a mate!

In 1966, a dinosaur skeleton was found in China that was covered in FUZZ. (Well, scientists call it "protofeathers.") The dinosaur is called Sinosauropteryx and it was so well preserved we can even tell that it had orange-and-white coloring!

Since it was found in China, here's its name in Chinese: 中华龙鸟

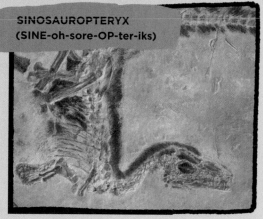

SINOSAUROPTERYX
(SINE-oh-sore-OP-ter-iks)

BUT MOST IMPORTANTLY → WHAT ABOUT T. REX?

Did T. rex have feathers?

Probably not. It might have had some areas of fuzz, but scientists believe that the mighty tyrannosaurus was covered in scales, not feathers.

However, we do know for sure that a cousin of T. rex had feathers.

YUTYRANNUS

Yutyrannus is the largest known dinosaur to be found with preserved evidence of feathers. It's estimated that Yutyrannuses were 30 feet long and weighed one and a half tons!

YUTYRANNUS
(YOO-tie-RAN-us)

DINOSAUR EGGS

Dinosaurs laid eggs just like birds do today. But their eggs had really thick shells!

When we think of an egg, it's shaped like this.

Some dinosaur eggs were almost perfectly round like a ball!

Some were elongated like a loaf of bread.

mommy?

A few fossilized embryos have been discovered still in their shells, but these are incredibly rare.

PROTOCERATOPS
(PRO-toe-SERRA-tops)
EGGS

TITANOSAUR
(tahy-tan-uh-sawr)
EGGS

OVIRAPTOR
(OH-vee-rap-t
EGGS

GIANT DINOS!

DIPLODOCUS
(DIP-lo-DOCK-us)

For a long time it was considered the longest dinosaur. It was roughly the size of four elephants. Go to page 16 to see a dinosaur that's MUCH longer!

CAMARASAURUS
(CAM-a-ra-SORE-us)

TINY HEADS

APATOSAURUS
(ah-PAT-oh-SORE-us)

THEY'RE _NOT_ MEAT EATERS, RIGHT?!

HUMAN

THIS REALLY IS HOW SMALL YOU WOULD BE!

HOW DID THEY GET SO BIG?

One reason is that they didn't chew their food! Yep, sauropods had teeth, but mostly used them to rake leaves and needles from trees. Mammals don't get as big as the sauropods, in part, because chewing requires a lot of energy.

THE SAUROPODS

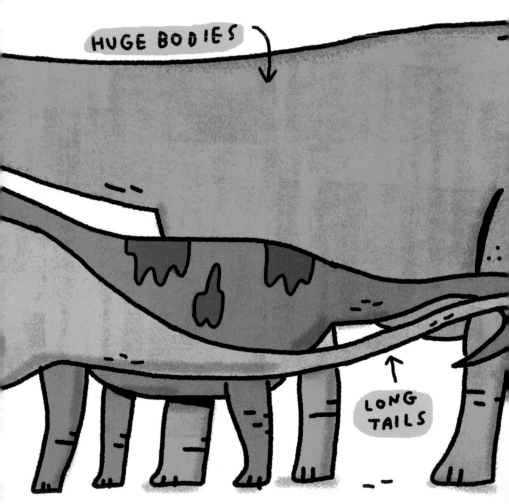

HUGE BODIES

LONG TAILS

These absolutely HUGE plant-eating dinosaurs first appeared in the late Triassic period and walked Earth for 140 million years. They had tiny heads, big bodies, and long necks that they used to get food from tall trees. Some had loooong tails that they may have been able to crack like a whip. Some even had a club at the end of their tail.

TITANOSAURS!

(tahy-tan-uh-sawrz)

THE **BIGGEST** DINOSAUR!

ARGENTINOSAUR
(ar-jen-TEEN-oh-SORE-us)
HERBIVORE

Titanosaurs included some supersized sauropods! By the end of the Cretaceous period, the titanosaurs were on every continent.

They could grow up to 121 feet long and weigh over 70 tons (140,000 pounds). That's TEN TIMES the weight of the biggest elephants on Earth today and longer than a 737 plane.

THE TITANOSAUR

TITANOSAUR

ONE OF tHE SMALLEST DINOSAURS EVER FOUND IS THE CROW-SIZED

DILONG. (DEE-long)

THEY SHOULD'VE CALLED IT THE **TINY**RANNOSAURUS!

← CARNIVORE

itanosaurs were some of the biggest nimals ever to walk on Earth, but they're ot the biggest animals ever on the planet. hat title belongs to the

BLUE WHALE →

HORNED DINOSAURS

HERBIVORE ↓

FOUND IN CANADA ↓

STYRACOSAURUS

STYRACOSAURUS
(stih-RAK-uh-SAWR-us)

(GREEK FOR "SPIKED LIZARD")

MAY HAVE BEEN FASTER THAN AN ELEPHANT!
(ABOUT 15 MILES PER HOUR.)

15 HORNS!

HERBIVORE ↓

KOSMOCERATOPS!
(KOS-mo-SERR-a-tops)

NAME MEANS "ORNATE HORN FACE" →

DEVELOPED All THIS WILD ORNAMENTATION TO ATTRACT A MATE ♥

KOSMOCERATOPS

TRICERATOPS

(try-SERR-ah-tops)

HERBIVORE

← 30 FEET LONG

AK LIKE A RROT

THEY WOULD CHARGE LIKE A RHINO!

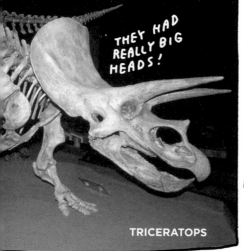

THEY HAD REALLY BIG HEADS!

TRICERATOPS

JOKE ALERT!

WHICH **DINOSAUR** NEVER GIVES UP? A **TRY**-CERATOPS!

AWESOME FACT!

Sure, the horns on these dinosaurs look...um...a little intimidating, but some scientists believe they might have been for attracting a mate, not for fighting off enemies. Whatever the reason, these dinosaurs had a bone that stuck out of their heads that was covered in a material called keratin, which was a lot like human fingernails!

ARMORED DINOSAURS!

These dinosaurs were covered in hard plates and spiky armor that they would use to protect themselves from predators.

ANTARCTOPELTA
(ann-TARK-toh-PEL-ta)

LOOKS LIKE IT SHOULD BREATHE FIRE, BUT IT DOESN'T.

13 FEET LONG

FOUND IN ANTARCTICA (MAYBE YOU COULD GUESS THAT?)

EDMONTONIA

CHECK OUT THAT HELMET

(ed-mon-TONE-ee-ah)

DIDN'T GET A CLUBBED TAIL! (AWW)

SOME HAD CLUBBED TAILS THAT COULD BREAK T.REX'S BONES!

ANKYLOSAURUS

THEY WERE BUILT LIKE PREHISTORIC TANKS!

6 FT TALL

5-6.5 TONS

SMALL BRAINS

ATE LOW-LYING PLANTS

(an-KILE-oh-SORE-us)

ANKYLOSAURUS

AWESOME FACT!

THEIR HEAD, NECK, AND TAIL WERE COVERED WITH HARD PLATES OF BONE CALLED OSTEODERMS.

WANNA RACE?

They were so heavy and low to the ground, they could only go about 6 miles per hour!

21

CONTRARY TO POPULAR BELIEF, the T. rex actually had really great eyesight (and they were fast enough to have caught humans if we had lived in the time of the dinosaurs)!

SO, THE T. REX WASN'T THE (BIGGEST) OR THE FASTEST DINOSAUR, **BUT** IT DID HA REALLY BIG TEETH

They could use their super-strong jaws to rip off over 500 pounds of meat from their prey with a single bite.

Their arms were only 3 feet long. That might seem little, but they weren't useless! It's believed that they were used to hold prey while eating or to SLASH prey if they got too close.

ITS TEETH WERE THE SIZE OF BANANAS!

THAT'S BANANAS.

BUT, UM, MUCH SHARPER.

More than 20 almost-complete T. rex skeletons have been found. The most intact one is named Sue.

TYRANNOSAURUS REX!

(tie-RAN-oh-SORE-us)

NAME MEANS:
"TYRANT LIZARD KING"

- COULD GROW 15-20 FEET TALL
- THEY HAD BIG BRAINS! (ABOUT TWICE AS BIG AS OTHER PREDATORS THEIR SIZE.)

TYRANNOSAURUS REX

AWESOME FACT!

They grew VERY QUICKLY. Between the ages of 14 and 18, they would put on an average of 5 pounds every single day.

JOKE ALERT!

WHAT IS SOMETHING T. REXES HAD THAT NO OTHER ANIMAL EVER HAD?

BABY T. REXES!

DINOSAUR BRAINS

THE SMARTEST DINOSAUR:

TROODON

(TROH-oh-don)

IT HAD AN UNUSUALLY LARGE BRAIN

that might have made it a little smarter than other dinosaurs, but still only about as smart as a chicken.

CARNIVORE ↗

Troodons had eyes set toward the front of their faces rather than on the sides of their heads. This gave them the ability to be better hunters.

Many herbivores had eyes on the sides of their heads so they could be better at noticing if a predator was approaching.

WHAT'S THAT SUPPOSED TO MEAN?!

WEIRD FACT →

One scientist speculated that if the Troodons weren't killed off in the mass extinction, they possibly could have evolved into intelligent creatures with bodies similar to humans... but of course this didn't really happen!

THE NOT-SO-SMARTEST DINOSAUR:

STEGOSAURUS

(steg-oh-SORE-us)

Okay, they probably weren't the dumbest dinosaurs, but they did have unusually small brains!

BRAIN THE SIZE OF A LIME!

THEIR SPIKED TAIL IS CALLED A THAGOMIZER!

HERBIVORE

THE STEGOSAURUS HAD SUCH A SMALL BRAIN THAT FOR A WHILE SOME PALEONTOLOGISTS BELIEVED THEY HAD EXTRA BRAIN MATTER IN THEIR HIP REGION!

(IT TURNED OUT TO JUST BE A POCKET OF EXTRA TISSUE.)

STEGOSAURUS

EVEN MORE DINOSAURS!

WEIRDEST LOOKIN' DINO

(Scientists have nicknamed them ELVISAURUSES because of that crazy crest thing on top of their heads.)

CARNIVORE

MAY HAVE HAD FEATHER

A HUNKA' HUNKA' BURNIN' LOVE

WEIGHED MORE THAN A POLAR BEAR

CRYOLOPHOSAURUS
(CRY-oh-LOFF-oh-SORE-us)

THE BIGGEST MEAT-EATING DINOSAUR ↓

SPINOSAURUS
(SPY-no-SORE-us)

ONE OF THE ONLY DINOS THAT COULD SWIM.

7-FOOT-TALL SPINES

MOSTLY ATE FISH.

COULD GROW UP TO 50 FEET LONG

PACHYCEPHALO-SAURUS

(PACK-ee-KEFF-a-low-SORE-us)

NAME MEANS: "THICK-HEADED LIZARD"!

It came from a group of dinosaurs called pachycephalosauridae, which all had thick, hard skulls. Some paleontologists think they used these thick skulls to head- butt one another, like bighorn sheep do, or for self-defense.

PACHYCEPHALOSAURUS

TOP OF SKULL WAS 10 INCHES THICK!

EXTINCTION:

WHAT HAPPENED?

65 MILLION YEARS AGO, SOMETHING KILLED THE DINOSAURS.

(AND THE PTEROSAURS, THE GIANT MARINE REPTILES, AND ABOUT **75%** OF ALL SPECIES ON EARTH)

IT'S CALLED THE **CRETACEOUS-PALEOGENE EXTINCTION EVENT.**

(AKA THE K-Pg EXTINCTION)

So what happened? Well, we don't know for sure, but scientists have a few theories.

THEORY ①

One theory is that volcanoes are to blame. There was a huge increase in volcanic eruptions, and all of that gas in the atmosphere could have trapped a lot of heat, making it too hot for the dinosaurs. OR, all of the volcanic eruptions caused ash and dust to fill the atmosphere, blocking out the sun.

THEORY ②

Another theory is that an asteroid 6 to 10 miles wide hit Earth. The impact would have caused dense clouds of dust all over the world to block out the sun. This would have killed off the plants, which would then kill off plant-eating dinosaurs and then dinosaur-eating dinosaurs.

JOKE ALERT!

WHAT IS A DINO'S LEAST FAVORITE REINDEER?

COMET

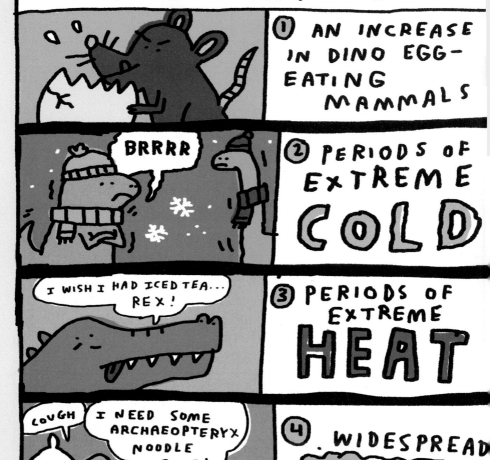

Or, it could have been a combination of a few of these theories! Whatever it was, it wasn't an overnight event. The extinction of the dinosaurs took place over thousands of years!

DIGGING FOR BONES

Dinosaurs left behind fossils. Stuff like:

BONES

TEETH

FOOTPRINTS

THEY EVEN LEFT BEHIND FOSSILIZED... UM...DROPPINGS!

HOW EMBARRASSING!

PALEONTOLOGIST**S**

ARE SCIENTISTS WHO STUDY

FOSSILS.

They hunt for bones on expeditions where they spend long days searching for signs left by the dinosaurs.

They also compare the fossils they find to living animals to find out what those dinosaurs could have been like. If a skeleton shows large, sharp teeth and thin limbs, we can assume that it was a carnivore that needed to move quickly to catch its prey.

DILOPHOSAURUS
(DIE-low-fo-SORE-us)

Piecing together all this stuff can be like putting together a really big puzzle with missing pieces and no picture to look at. In fact, there have been some pretty odd assumptions made by scientists in the past. Not because they weren't smart, but because they didn't have all the information we have today.

AMBER

Scientists have even found a piece of a dinosaur tail trapped in ancient, harden tree sap called amber. Are you wondering if the piece dinosaur tail had feathers? It did!

BONUS
- - - -
FACT!

One of the biggest bones ever found is the backbone of an Argentinosaurus. It was 5 ft. by 5 ft. and weighed more than a TON.

KEEP YOUR EYES PEELED ... AND YOU MIGHT DISCOVER A DINOSAUR FOSSIL SOMEDAY!